KATE RIGGS

grow with me

BUTTERFLY

CREATIVE EDUCATION

Published by Creative Education
P.O. Box 227, Mankato, Minnesota 56002
Creative Education is an imprint of
The Creative Company
www.thecreativecompany.us

Design and production by Ellen Huber
Art direction by Rita Marshall
Printed in the United States of America

Photographs by Dreamstime (Cameramannz,
Melinda Fawver, Deborah Hewitt, Suenorth), Getty
Images (Ingo Arndt, Oxford Scientific, Dannie Quinn,
Patricio Robles Gil/Sierra Madre, Joel Sartore,
Kim Taylor and Jane Burton), iStockphoto (arlindo71,
Jacob Hamblin, malerapaso, Alexander Omelko,
Joe Pogliano), National Geographic (Thomas
Marent/Minden Pictures), Photo Researchers (Scott
Camazine, Stuart Wilson), Shutterstock (Anat-oli,
hagit berkovich, Ziga Camernik, D. Kucharski &
K. Kucharska, Shani Rubin-Pinhas), SuperStock
(Minden Pictures, NHPA), Veer (Vladimir Blinov,
Golfkatze, ncousla, peterwey, smithore, Mihail Zhukov)

Library of Congress Cataloging-in-Publication Data
Riggs, Kate.
Butterfly / Kate Riggs.
p. cm. — (Grow with me)
Includes bibliographical references and index.
Summary: An exploration of the life cycle and life
span of butterflies, using up-close photographs and
step-by-step text to follow a butterfly's growth process
from egg to larva to pupa to mature insect.

ISBN 978-1-60818-215-2
1. Butterflies—Life cycles—Juvenile literature. I. Title.
QL544.2.R54 2012
595.789—dc23   2011040496

First Edition
9 8 7 6 5 4 3 2 1

TABLE OF CONTENTS

Butterflies are insects. Insects have six legs and one or two pairs of wings. Butterflies have two pairs of wings. Their wings and legs are connected to the part of their body called the **thorax**.

thorax

4

Butterflies live in many places around the world. They can live in forests, deserts, grasslands, and mountains. They do not have nests or **permanent** homes. Many butterflies **migrate** in the spring and fall. If adult butterflies stay in one place year round, they may **hibernate** in holes in trees or other safe places.

Monarch butterflies migrate to warm places such as Mexico in the fall.

5

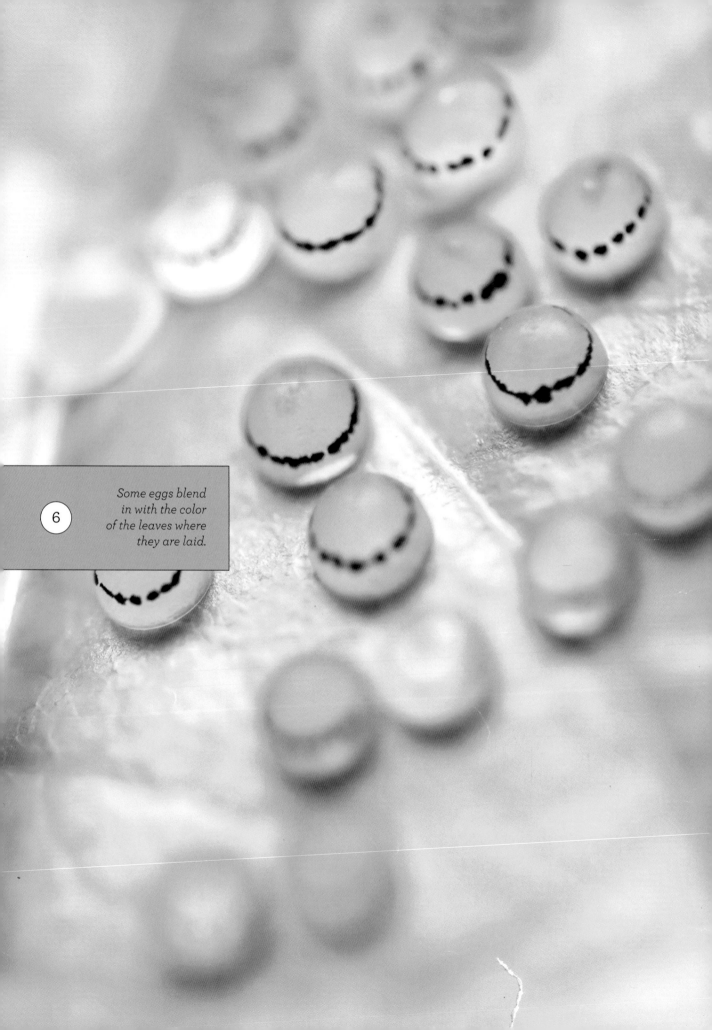

Some eggs blend
in with the color
of the leaves where
they are laid.

6

The red admiral butterfly lays its eggs on the leaves of plants called nettles.

7

Female butterlies lay their eggs on plant leaves. All the eggs are covered on the outside by a shell called a chorion (*COR-ee-on*). A special glue helps the egg stick to the leaf.

Some butterfly **species** lay many eggs on a leaf. Some lay just one egg at a time. A butterfly can lay fewer than 100 or more than 1,000 eggs a year.

Most butterflies lay their eggs when it is warm outside. Butterflies are cold-blooded. This means they cannot keep their bodies warm if the temperature around them is not also warm.

8

To fly, a butterfly's body needs to be at a temperature of 82 to 102 °F (28 to 39 °C). If the weather is too cold, a butterfly has to warm itself in the sun. Then it can fly and lay its eggs.

Owl butterflies live in warm forests and lay tiny white eggs.

These monarch butterflies stay in the sun to keep warm.

A caterpillar's first meal is its eggshell. It eats its way out of the egg.

Inside the egg, a butterfly **larva** is growing. It grows for about two weeks before it hatches. If an egg is laid late in the fall, the larva stays inside until spring comes. It does not want to hatch when the weather is too cold.

A butterfly larva is called a caterpillar. Caterpillars can be many different colors. Some have stripes or other **patterns**. A caterpillar is long and looks like a worm. It does not have wings, but it does have legs and a mouth.

11

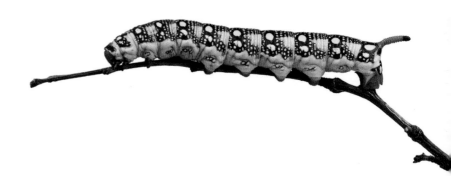

A caterpillar spends all day eating food. Most caterpillars eat only plants. But some may eat insects, too. A caterpillar spends about two weeks eating.

12

Caterpillars shed their skin, or molt, as they grow. This happens four or five times. Molting helps a caterpillar fit into the bigger body it will need as a butterfly.

Monarch caterpillars eat the leaves of a plant called milkweed.

13

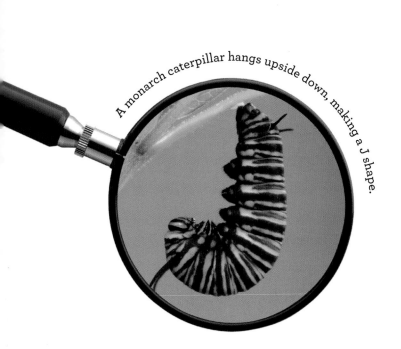

A monarch caterpillar hangs upside down, making a J shape.

14 After it has finished growing, a caterpillar looks for a place to rest. It spins **silk** threads to attach itself under a leaf or onto a plant stem. Then it hangs upside down. Some caterpillars spin silk around their bodies and hang with their heads up instead.

Then the caterpillar molts for the last time. It makes a hard outer covering for itself. The larva starts to change into a **pupa**. A butterfly pupa is called a chrysalis (*KRIS-ah-lis*). Some pupae spend the winter as chrysalises.

This caterpillar is molting for the last time and becoming a pupa.

15

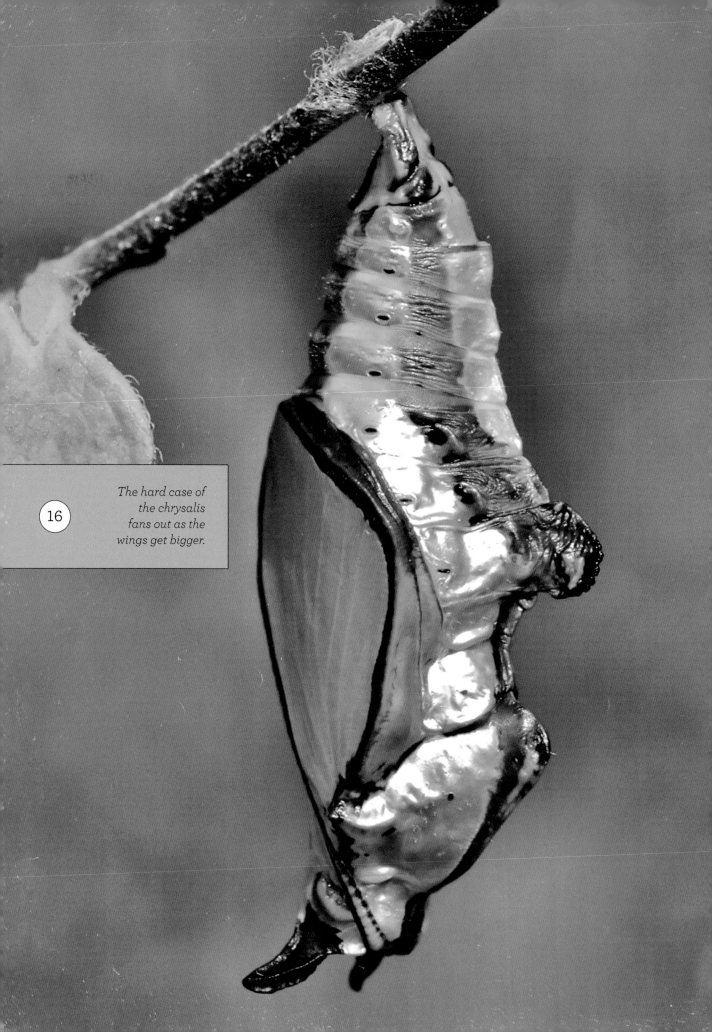

The hard case of the chrysalis fans out as the wings get bigger.

16

The chrysalis cannot move. It stays on the leaf or stem for one week or longer. The chrysalis is brown, green, or gray. It blends in with the plants around it. This helps it hide from animals that might want to eat it.

As a chrysalis, the pupa's wings begin to grow. The pupa's body changes from looking like a caterpillar to looking like an adult butterfly.

17

Some chrysalises become see-through right before the pupa is done growing.

When the wings are fully grown, a butterfly climbs up out of the chrysalis. An adult butterfly is called an imago (*ih-MAY-goh*).

The imago cannot use its wings right away. It hangs onto the leaf or stem and waits. Its body pumps blood into the wings to make them move. Then the wings have to dry.

18

A monarch hangs upside down and comes out of the chrysalis head first.

A swallowtail imago leaves its case and waits for its wings to harden.

19

This malachite butterfly holds its colorful wings up in the air.

Touching a butterfly's wings will rub off some of its scales, but it can still fly.

21

After one to three hours, the imago's wings harden and unfold. Now the imago can fly. When the butterfly lands to rest, the wings stick straight up in the air.

Butterfly wings are covered with tiny scales. Most scales are colored brown or black. The two front wings are called forewings. The two back wings are called hindwings.

Some butterflies live only two to six weeks. Others live as long as six to eight months. They feed mostly on **nectar** in flowers. A butterfly uses a long mouthpart called a proboscis (*pro-BAH-sis*) to suck up nectar and other liquids.

To find nectar, a butterfly uses its **antennae**. The antennae stick out from the butterfly's head. They pick up scents, or smells, in the air. The smells that flowers make lead a butterfly to their nectar.

22

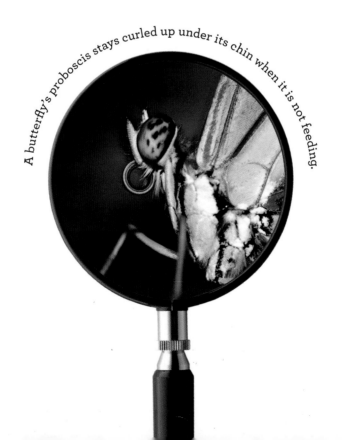

A butterfly's proboscis stays curled up under its chin when it is not feeding.

Butterflies get nectar from many flowering plants, including dandelions.

23

24

Female butterflies are usually larger than males and tend to live longer.

An adult butterfly spends its time finding a mate. Male and female butterflies give off scents that attract each other. These smells let other butterflies know they are ready to mate.

Butterflies that live only a few weeks have to find their mates quickly. Then the females lay as many eggs as they can before they die. Butterflies that live longer may migrate after they mate. Monarch butterflies migrate. They lay their eggs as they fly to a warmer place.

25

Small creatures such as mantises (pictured) and spiders eat butterflies.

The butterflies that migrate usually live the longest. Many monarch butterflies spend the winter in warmer places. They can live for six to eight months.

Other butterflies stay in the same place their entire lives. They keep drinking nectar and mating. Then the females lay their eggs under a plant or on a leaf. A female chooses an egg-laying spot by "tasting" the leaf with her feet.

26

A butterfly's sense of taste is in its feet, not its mouth.

Many monarchs clump together on the ground when it is too cold for them to fly.

Caterpillars have three pairs of true legs near their heads.

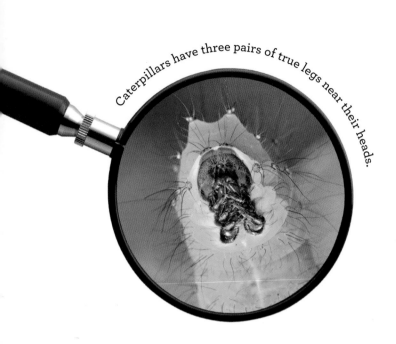

28 After a few days, weeks, or months, the butterflies get old and tired. When the males stop mating and the females stop laying eggs, they die. The larvae keep growing inside the eggs. These larvae will become chrysalises, and then they will turn into beautiful butterflies.

It takes a swallowtail pupa one to two weeks to become a butterfly.

The female butterfly lays her eggs on a leaf or plant stem.

A larva (caterpillar) begins growing in the egg.

The caterpillar hatches from the egg in about 2 weeks.

The caterpillar sheds its skin 4 or 5 times.

 After 2 to 4 weeks, the caterpillar is fully grown.

The caterpillar molts for the last time and changes into a pupa (chrysalis).

The chrysalis rests for 10 days or longer.

The adult butterfly (imago) leaves  the chrysalis and soon flies.

After about 2 to 6 weeks or 8 months, the imago dies.

antennae: *the pair of long, thin sense organs attached to a butterfly's head; "antenna" is the word for a single one*

hibernate: *to spend the winter sleeping or not moving around much*

larva: *the form a butterfly takes after it hatches but before it has skin and wings; "larvae" is the word for more than one larva*

migrate: *to move from place to place during different parts of the year, usually to find food and warmth*

nectar: *a sweet, sugary liquid that flowers make*

patterns: *lines or shapes that are repeated*

permanent: *lasting for a long time*

pupa: *the form a butterfly takes as it changes from larva to adult; "pupae" is the word for more than one pupa*

silk: *a thin, strong, soft material spun by larvae*

species: *groups of living things that are closely related*

thorax: *the middle part of an insect's body, between the head and the abdomen*

WEB SITES

Butterfly Activities for Kids
http://www.foremostbutterflies.com/butterfly_activities/
Print out activity pages to learn more about butterflies.

Enchanted Learning: Butterfly and Caterpillar Crafts
http://www.enchantedlearning.com/crafts/butterfly/
Learn how to make puppets, hanging mobiles, and more.

READ MORE

Heiligman, Deborah. *From Caterpillar to Butterfly*. New York: HarperCollins, 1996.

Murawski, Darlyne. *Face to Face with Caterpillars*. Washington, D.C.: National Geographic, 2007.

32